The Essential GITA

68 KEY VERSES *from the* BHAGAVAD GITA

MANDALA
PUBLISHING
PO Box 3088
San Rafael, CA 94912
www.mandalapublishing.com

Library of Congress
Cataloging-in-Publication Data available.

ISBN: 978-1-932771-03-9

Manufactured in China by Insight Editions.

10 9 8 7 6 5 4

The Essential GITA

68 KEY VERSES *from the* BHAGAVAD GITA

MANDALA
PUBLISHING

San Rafael, California

Contents

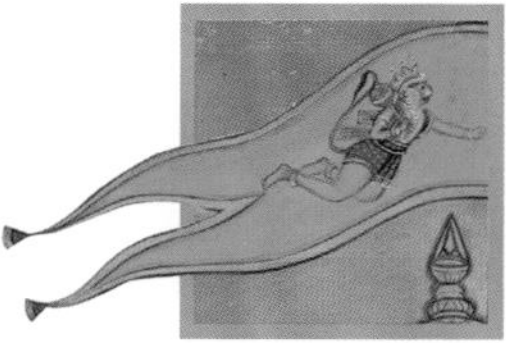

Invocation

CHAPTER 9, VERSE 2

राजविद्या राजगुह्यं पवित्रमिदमुत्तमम् ।
प्रत्यक्षावगमं धर्म्यं सुसुखं कर्तुमव्ययम् ॥२॥

rāja-vidyā rāja-guhyaṁ
pavitram idam uttamam
pratyakṣāvagamaṁ dharmyaṁ
susukhaṁ kartum avyayam

This knowledge is the king of education, the rarest of all secrets and the purest knowledge. Because it gives direct perception of the self by realization, it is the perfection of religion. It is eternal and joyfully performed.

Introduction

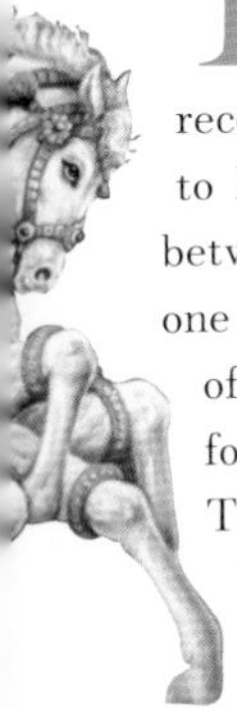

The Bhagavad Gita is the spiritual essence of India's great epic, the Mahabharata. The *Mahabharata* recounts the story of a great conflict said to have taken place some 5,000 years ago between two branches of a ruling family, one pious, the other wicked. The climax of the epic is the momentous battle fought by the two sides at Kurukshetra. The Bhagavad Gita is the conversation between Lord Krishna and his warrior friend, the pious prince Arjuna. It is spoken before the outbreak of this battle, in which the Lord inspires Arjuna with courage by clearly placing his life and duty within the cosmic order of the universe.

Being an enlightened associate of Lord Krishna, Arjuna was above illusion. On the battlefield, however, he was thrust into confusion, causing him to ask Krishna questions about the problems of life. Krishna's answers were meant not just for the benefit of Arjuna, but for all generations to come. Krishna told him how to overcome life's obstacles, allowing anyone who reads the Gita the wisdom to gain spiritual perfection in this life. The Gita is meant to liberate one from the bodily concept of life by explaining the science of the soul and its relation to the Absolute and matter. By developing the power to discriminate between temporary matter and eternal spiritual truths, one can achieve the ultimate goal of devotion to God. All the instructions in the Gita are intended to awaken our pure consciousness, thus enabling us to enter the highest realms of spiritual attainment.

The Gita was unknown in the Western world until the end of the 18th century, but since then it has influenced many of its greatest thinkers. Philosophers like Kant, Hegel, and Schopenhauer, the American transcendentalists Emerson and

Thoreau, and scientists like Einstein and Oppenheimer have taken inspiration from the Gita's eternal wisdom.

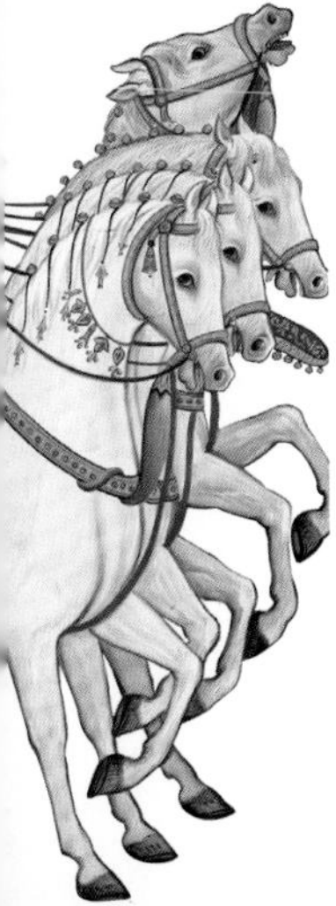

Nature

SEED *of* CREATION

CHAPTER 7, VERSES 9–10

पुण्यो गन्धः पृथिव्यां च तेजश्चास्मि विभावसौ ।
ज वनं सर्वभूतेषु तपश्चास्मि तपस्विषु ॥९॥
ब जं मां सर्वभूतानां विद्धि पार्थ सनातनम् ।
बुद्धिर्बुद्धिमतामस्मि तेजस्तेजस्विनामहम् ॥१०॥

puṇyo gandhaḥ pṛthivyāṁ ca
tejaś cāsmi vibhāvasau
jīvanaṁ sarva-bhūteṣu
tapaś cāsmi tapasviṣu

I am the original fragrance of the earth; I am the heat in fire and the life in all living things; I am the ascetic's inner spiritual fire. Know Me to be the seed of all creation, original and eternal. I am the intelligence of the intelligent and the effulgence of all great and powerful persons.

the Sacred Om

Chapter 7, Verse 8

रसोऽहमप्सु कौन्तेय प्रभास्मि शशिसूर्ययोः ।
प्रणवः सर्ववेदेषु शब्दः खे पौरुषं नृषु ॥८॥

raso'ham apsu kaunteya
prabhāsmi śaśi-sūryayoḥ
praṇavaḥ sarva-vedeṣu
śabdaḥ khe pauruṣaṁ nṛṣu

I am the fresh taste of water, the light of the sun and moon; I am the sacred syllable *om* in the Vedic mantras, the sound in ether, and the ability in man.

PEARLS *on a* THREAD

CHAPTER 7, VERSES 6–7

एतद्योन नि भूतानि सर्वाण त्युपधारय ।
अहं कृत्स्नस्य जगतः प्रभवः प्रलयस्तथा ॥६॥
मत्तः परतरं नान्यत् किञ्चिदस्ति धनञ्जय ।
मयि सर्वमिदं प्रोतं सूत्रे मणिगणा इव ॥७॥

etad-yonīni bhūtāni
sarvāṇīty upadhāraya
ahaṁ kṛtsnasya jagataḥ
prabhavaḥ pralayas tathā

Know for certain that whatever is found in this creation arises out of a combination of my material and spiritual energies. I am the origin and dissolution of all. There is nothing beyond Me, Arjuna. Everything rests upon Me as pearls are strung on a thread.

Material Elements

Chapter 7, Verse 4

भूमिरापोऽनलो वायुः खं मनो बुद्धिरेव च ।
अहङ्कार इत यं मे भिन्ना प्रकृतिरष्टधा ॥४॥

bhūmir āpo'nalo vāyuḥ
khaṁ mano buddhir eva ca
ahaṁkāra itīyaṁ me
bhinnā prakṛtir aṣṭadhā

My material nature is made up of eight separate energies: earth, water, fire, air, ether, mind, intelligence, and false ego.

False Ego

Chapter 3, Verse 27

प्रकृतेः क्रियमाणानि गुणैः कर्माणि सर्वशः ।
अहंकारविमूढात्मा कर्ताहमिति मन्यते ॥२७॥

prakṛteḥ kriyamāṇāni
guṇaiḥ karmāṇi sarvaśaḥ
ahaṁkāra-vimūḍhātmā
kartāham iti manyate

Bewildered spirit souls, under the influence of the three modes of material nature, think themselves to be the doer of activities, which are in actuality carried out by nature.

SPARK *of* SPLENDOR

CHAPTER 10, VERSE 41

यद्यद्विभूतिमत्सत्त्वं श्र मदूर्जितमेव वा ।
तत्तदेवावगच्छ त्वं मम तेजोंऽशसम्भवम् ॥४१॥

yad yad vibhūtimat sattvaṁ
śrīmad ūrjitam eva vā
tat tad evāvagaccha tvaṁ
mama tejo'ṁśasaṁbhavam

Know that all beautiful, glorious
and mighty creations spring from
but a spark of My splendor.

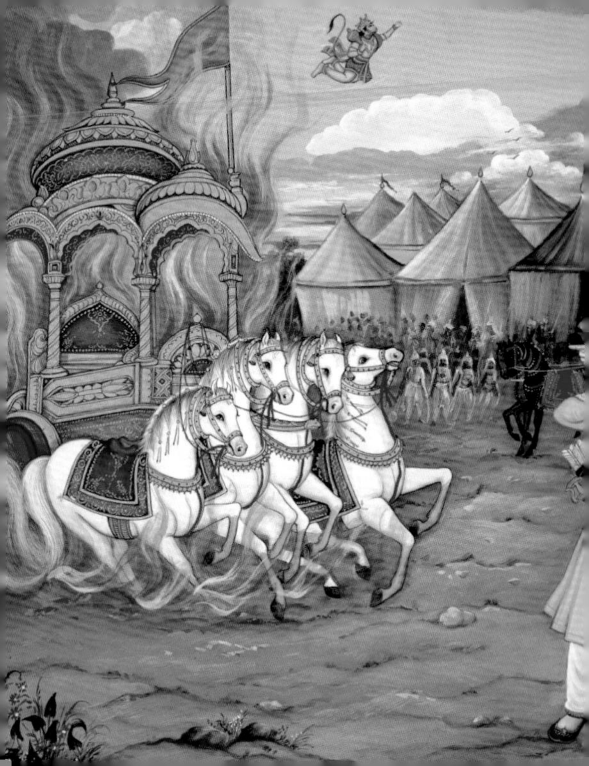

Desire

Sense Control

Chapter 2, Verse 58

यदा संहरते चायं कूर्मोऽङ्गान व सर्वशः ।
इन्द्रियाण न्द्रियार्थेभ्यस्तस्य प्रज्ञा प्रतिष्ठिता ॥५८॥

yadā saṁharate cāyaṁ
kūrmo'ṅgānīva sarvaśaḥ
indriyāṇīndriyārthebhyas
tasya prajñā pratiṣṭhitā

One who is able to withdraw the senses from their objects, like a tortoise drawing its limbs within its shell, is firmly established in wisdom.

THREE MODES

CHAPTER 14, VERSE 5

सत्त्वं रजस्तम इति गुणाः प्रकृतिसम्भवाः ।
निबध्नन्ति महाबाहो देहे देहिनमव्ययम् ॥५॥

sattvaṁ rajas tama iti
guṇāḥ prakṛti-saṁbhavāḥ
nibadhnanti mahā-bāho
dehe dehinam avyayam

There are three modes of material nature: goodness, passion, and ignorance. Though the living being is imperishable, he is bound in the body by these three modes.

Covered Soul

Chapter 3, Verse 38

धूमेनाव्रियते वह्निर्यथादर्शो मलेन च ।
यथोल्बेनावृतो गर्भस्तथा तेनेदमावृतम् ॥३८॥

dhūmenāvriyate vahnir
yathādarśo malena ca
yatholbenāvṛto garbhas
tathā tenedam āvṛtam

As fire is covered by smoke, as a mirror is covered by dust, or as the embryo is covered by the womb, similarly, the living being is covered by different layers of lust.

Conquering Lust

Chapter 3, Verse 43

एवं बुद्धेः परं बुद्ध्वा संस्तभ्यात्मानमात्मना ।
जहि शत्रुं महाबाहो कामरूपं दुरासदम् ॥४३॥

evaṁ buddheḥ paraṁ buddhvā
saṁstabhyātmānam ātmanā
jahi śatruṁ mahā-bāho
kāma-rūpaṁ durāsadam

Knowing the self to be transcendental to the intelligence, one should control the lower self by the higher self and thus, by spiritual strength, defeat this elusive enemy known as lust.

Pretenders

Chapter 3, Verse 6

कर्मेन्द्रियाणि संयम्य य आस्ते मनसा स्मरन् ।
इन्द्रियार्थान्विमूढात्मा मिथ्याचारः स उच्यते ॥६॥

karmendriyāṇi saṁyamya
ya āste manasā smaran
indriyārthān vimūḍhātmā
mithyācāraḥ sa ucyate

Those who restrain the working senses but continue to dwell on sense objects delude themselves and are called pretenders.

Conscious Entity

Chapter 13, Verse 34

यथा प्रकाशयत्येकः कृत्स्नं लोकमिमं रविः ।
क्षेत्रं क्षेत्र तथा कृत्स्नं प्रकाशयति भारत ॥३४॥

yathā prakāśayaty ekaḥ
kṛtsnaṁ lokam imaṁ raviḥ
kṣetraṁ kṣetrī tathā kṛtsnaṁ
prakāśayati bhārata

Those whose minds are enchanted by sense enjoyment and material opulence never find the resolute determination to practice spiritual life.

WINDS *of* DESIRE

CHAPTER 2, VERSE 67

इन्द्रियाणां हि चरतां यन्मनोऽनुविध यते ।
तदस्य हरति प्रज्ञां वायुर्नावमिवाम्भसि ॥६७॥

indriyāṇāṁ hi caratāṁ
yan mano'nuvidhīyate
tad asya harati prajñāṁ
vāyur nāvam ivāmbhasi

As a boat on water is swept
away by a strong wind and thrown
off course, even one of the senses
on which the mind focuses can
carry away one's intelligence.

Determination

Chapter 2, Verse 44

भोगैश्वर्यप्रसक्तानां तयापहृतचेतसाम् ।
व्यवसायात्मिका बुद्धिः समाधौ न विध यते ॥४४॥

bhogaiśvarya-prasaktānāṁ
tayāpahṛta-cetasām
vyavasāyātmikā buddhiḥ
samādhau na vidhīyate

Those too attached to sense enjoyment and material opulence are enchanted by the scriptural promises of such things. They can never find the resolute determination to perfect their spiritual life.

WOMBS *of* MISERY

CHAPTER 5, VERSE 22

ये हि संस्पर्शजा भोगा दुःखयोनय एव ते ।
आद्यन्तवन्तः कौन्तेय न तेषु रमते बुधः ॥२२॥

ye hi saṁsparśa-jā bhogā
duḥkha-yonaya eva te
ādy-anta-vantaḥ kaunteya
na teṣu ramate budhaḥ

The pleasures that derive from contact with sense objects are the wombs of misery. They have both a beginning and an end and thus the wise take no delight in them.

GATES *to* HELL

CHAPTER 16, VERSE 21

त्रिविधं नरकस्येदं द्वारं नाशनमात्मनः।
कामः क्रोधस्तथा लोभस्तस्मादेतत्त्रयं त्यजेत् ॥२१॥

tri-vidhaṁ narakasyedaṁ
dvāraṁ nāśanam ātmanaḥ
kāmaḥ krodhas tathā lobhas
tasmād etat trayaṁ tyajet

There are three gates that open the way to hell and the degradation of the soul: lust, anger, and greed. Avoid these three at all costs, O Arjuna.

Our Enemy

Chapter 3, Verses 36–37

अर्जुन उवाच
अथ केन प्रयुक्तोऽयं पापं चरति पूरुषः ।
अनिच्छन्नपि वार्ष्णेय बलादिव नियोजितः ॥३६॥

arjuna uvāca
atha kena prayukto'yaṁ
pāpaṁ carati pūruṣaḥ
anicchann api vārṣṇeya
balād iva niyojitaḥ

Arjuna asked: By what is one impelled to sin, even unwillingly, as if engaged by force? Krishna replied: It is lust alone, born of the mode of passion and later transformed into anger. It is the mighty, all-devouring source of sin, and the true enemy of this world.

All-knowing One

Chapter 7, Verse 26

वेदाहं समत तानि वर्तमानानि चार्जुन ।
भविष्याणि च भूतानि मां तु वेद न कश्चन ॥२६॥

vedāhaṁ samatītāni
vartamānāni cārjuna
bhaviṣyāṇi ca bhūtāni
māṁ tu veda na kaścana

I know all beings in the creation as they were in the past, as they are now, and as they shall one day come to be, yet not one of them knows Me in full. O Arjuna, all living entities are born into illusion, overcome by the duality of desire and hate.

B. G. Sharma

Meditation

Protection

Chapter 9, Verse 22

अनन्याश्चिन्तयन्तो मां ये जनाः पर्युपासते ।
तेषां नित्याभियुक्तानां योगक्षेमं वहाम्यहम् ॥२२॥

ananyāś cintayanto māṁ
ye janāḥ paryupāsate
teṣāṁ nityābhiyuktānāṁ
yoga-kṣemaṁ vahāmy aham

For those who worship Me
with devotion, meditating
on My transcendental form,
I carry what they lack and
preserve what they have, both
materially and spiritually.

Calm Meditation

Chapter 6, Verse 19

यथा द पो निवातस्थो नेङ्गते सोपमा स्मृता ।
योगिनो यतचित्तस्य युञ्जतो योगमात्मनः ॥१९॥

yathā dīpo nivāta-stho
neṅgate sopamā smṛtā
yogino yata-cittasya
yuñjato yogam ātmanaḥ

As a lamp in a windless place does not waver, so the yogi whose mind is focused remains always steady in meditation on the transcendent Self.

Intelligence

Chapter 3, Verse 42

इन्द्रियाणि पराण्याहुरिन्द्रियेभ्यः परं मनः ।
मनसस्तु परा बुद्धिर्यो बुद्धेः परतस्तु सः ॥४२॥

indriyāṇi parāṇy āhur
indriyebhyaḥ paraṁ manaḥ
manasas tu parā buddhir
yo buddheḥ paratas tu saḥ

The senses are superior
to matter; mind is higher than
the senses. Higher than the
mind is intelligence, but
the soul is higher still.

OFFERINGS *of* DEVOTION

CHAPTER 9, VERSES 26–27

पत्रं पुष्पं फलं तोयं यो मे भक्त्या प्रयच्छति ।
तदहं भक्त्युपहृतमश्नामि प्रयतात्मनः ॥२६॥
यत्करोषि यदश्नासि यज्जुहोषि ददासि यत् ।
यत्तपस्यसि कौन्तेय तत्कुरुष्व मदर्पणम् ॥२७॥

patraṁ puṣpaṁ phalaṁ toyaṁ
yo me bhaktyā prayacchati
tad ahaṁ bhakty-upahṛtam
aśnāmi prayatātmanaḥ

If one offers Me with love and devotion a flower, a fruit, a leaf, or even water, I accept it. Whatever you do or eat, whatever you offer or give away, whatever austerities you perform, do as an offering unto Me.

Forest *of* Delusion

Chapter 2, Verse 52

यदा ते मोहकलिलं बुद्धिर्व्यतितरिष्यति ।
तदा गन्तासि निर्वेदं श्रोतव्यस्य श्रुतस्य च ॥५२॥
श्रुतिविप्रतिपन्ना ते यदा स्थास्यति निश्चला ।
समाधावचला बुद्धिस्तदा योगमवाप्स्यसि ॥५३॥

yadā te moha-kalilaṁ
buddhir vyatitariṣyati
tadā gantāsi nirvedaṁ
śrotavyasya śrutasya ca

When your intelligence has passed beyond the dense forest of confusion, you shall become indifferent to all scriptural injunctions in the past or the future.

Pure Devotees

Chapter 10, Verse 9

मच्चित्ता मद्गतप्राणा बोधयन्तः परस्परम् ।
कथयन्तश्च मां नित्यं तुष्यन्ति च रमन्ति च ॥९॥

mac-cittā mad-gata-prāṇā
bodhayantaḥ parasparam
kathayantaś ca māṁ nityaṁ
tuṣyanti ca ramanti ca

The thoughts of My pure devotees dwell in Me, their lives are surrendered to Me, and they derive great satisfaction and joy enlightening one another and speaking about Me.

Friend *or* Enemy

Chapter 6, Verse 6

बन्धुरात्मात्मनस्तस्य येनात्मैवात्मना जितः ।
अनात्मनस्तु शत्रुत्वे वर्तेतात्मैव शत्रुवत् ॥६॥

bandhur ātmātmanas tasya
yenātmaivātmanā jitaḥ
anātmanas tu śatrutve
vartetātmaiva śatruvat

For one who has controlled the mind, it is the best of friends, but for one who has failed to do so, it remains the greatest enemy.

TOLERANCE

CHAPTER 2, VERSE 14

मात्रास्पर्शस्तु कौन्तेय शितोष्णसुखदुःखदाः ।
आगमापायिनोऽनित्यास्तांस्तितिक्षस्व भारत ॥१४॥

mātrā-sparśās tu kaunteya
śītoṣṇa-sukha-duḥkhadāḥ
āgamāpāyino'nityās
tāṁs titikṣasva bhārata

The temporary appearance of happiness and distress, and their disappearance over time, are like the coming and going of winter and summer seasons. They arise from sense perception and one must learn to tolerate them without being disturbed.

Immovable Himalayas

Chapter 10, Verse 25

महर्षीणां भृगुरहं गिरामस्म्येकमक्षरम् ।
यज्ञानां जपयज्ञोऽस्मि स्थावराणां हिमालयः ॥२५॥

maharṣīṇāṁ bhṛgur ahaṁ
girām asmy ekam akṣaram
yajñānāṁ japa-yajño'smi
sthāvarāṇāṁ himālayaḥ

Of the great seers I am Bhrigu; of words, I am the syllable *om*. Of sacrifices I am *japa*, the silent chanting of the Holy Names, and among immovable things, I am the Himalayan Mountains.

the Supersoul

Chapter 15, Verse 15

वेदैश्च सर्वैरहमेव वेद्यो
वेदान्तकृद् वेदविदेव चाहम् ॥१५॥

sarvasya cāhaṁ hṛdi sanniviṣṭo
mattaḥ smṛtir jñānam apohanaṁ ca
vedaiś ca sarvair aham eva vedyo
vedānta-kṛd veda-vid eva cāham

I reside in every heart. From Me alone come remembrance, knowledge, and forgetfulness. I am to be known by all the Vedas. I am the author of the Vedanta and I alone know the Vedas.

Seeing God

Chapter 6, Verse 30

यो मां पश्यति सर्वत्र सर्वं च मयि पश्यति ।
तस्याहं न प्रणश्यामि स च मे न प्रणश्यति ॥३०॥

yo māṁ paśyati sarvatra
sarvaṁ ca mayi paśyati
tasyāhaṁ na praṇaśyāmi
sa ca me na praṇaśyati

Those who see Me in all things, and all things in Me, are never lost to Me, nor am I ever lost to them.

Yoga

Fall *from* Grace

Chapter 2, Verses 62–63

ध्यायतो विषयान् पुंसः सङ्गस्तेषूपजायते ।
सङ्गात् सञ्जायते कामः कामात् क्रोधोऽभिजायते ॥६२॥
क्रोधाद्भवति सम्मोहः सम्मोहात् स्मृतिविभ्रमः ।
स्मृतिभ्रंशाद् बुद्धिनाशो बुद्धिनाशात् प्रणश्यति ॥६३॥

dhyāyato viṣayān puṁsaḥ
saṅgas teṣūpajāyate
saṅgāt saṁjāyate kāmaḥ
kāmāt krodho'bhijāyate

One who contemplates the sense objects becomes attachment to them. From attachment develops lust and then anger. From anger confusion is born, which results in memory loss. When memory is bewildered, intelligence is lost, leading one again into material conciousness.

Maintaining Balance

Chapter 6, Verse 16

नात्यश्नतस्तु योगोऽस्ति न चैकान्तमनश्नतः ।
न चातिस्वप्नश लस्य जाग्रतो नैव चार्जुन ॥१६॥

nātyaśnatas tu yogo'sti
na caikāntam anaśnataḥ
na cātisvapna-śīlasya
jāgrato naiva cārjuna

One can have no success in yoga if one eats too much or eats too little. Nor can one be successful if one sleeps too much or does not sleep enough.

Best *of* Yogis

Chapter 6, Verse 47

योगिनामपि सर्वेषां मद्गतेनान्तरात्मना ।
श्रद्धावान् भजते यो मां स मे युक्ततमो मतः ॥४७॥

yogināṁ api sarveṣāṁ
mad-gatenāntarātmanā
śraddhāvān bhajate yo māṁ
sa me yuktatamo mataḥ

Of all yogis, the one who is filled with faith, his entire being given over to Me, is the most intimately united with Me and is the best of all.

the Restless Mind

Chapter 6, Verse 36

असंयतात्मना योगो दुष्प्राप इति मे मतिः ।
वश्यात्मना तु यतता शक्योऽवाप्तुमुपायतः ॥३६॥

asaṁyatātmanā yogo
duṣprāpa iti me matiḥ
vaśyātmanā tu yatatā
śakyo'vāptum upāyataḥ

The yoga practitioner whose mind is unbridled can never attain self-realization. Only one who has mastered the self and who strives by right means is assured of success.

Success *in* Yoga

Chapter 2, Verse 48

योगस्थः कुरु कर्माणि सङ्गं त्यक्त्वा धनञ्जय ।
सिद्ध्यसिद्ध्योः समो भूत्वा समत्वं योग उच्यते ॥४८॥

yogasthaḥ kuru karmāṇi
saṅgaṁ tyaktvā dhanaṁjaya
siddhy-asiddhyoḥ samo bhūtvā
samatvaṁ yoga ucyate

Be steadfast in yoga, O Arjuna.
Perform your duty without attachment,
remaining equal to success or failure.
Such equanimity of mind is called yoga.

Overcoming Fear

Chapter 2, Verse 40

नेहाभिक्रमनाशोऽस्ति प्रत्यवायो न विद्यते ।
स्वल्पमप्यस्य धर्मस्य त्रायते महतो भयात् ॥४०॥

nehābhikrama-nāśo'sti
pratyavāyo na vidyate
svalpam apy asya dharmasya
trāyate mahato bhayāt

No effort on the yoga path is ever lost, nor can any obstacle ever hold one back forever. Just a little progress on this path can protect one from the greatest fear.

Sacrifice

Chapter 3, Verse 9

यज्ञार्थात् कर्मणोऽन्यत्र लोकोऽयं कर्मबन्धनः ।
तदर्थं कर्म कौन्तेय मुक्तसङ्गः समाचर ॥९॥

yajñārthāt karmaṇo’nyatra
loko’yaṁ karma-bandhanaḥ
tad-arthaṁ karma kaunteya
mukta-saṅgaḥ samācara

Any action that is not performed as a sacrifice to God is a source of bondage to this material world. Therefore carry out your prescribed duties as a sacrifice, remaining unattached to the results.

Rare Souls

Chapter 7, Verse 3

मनुष्याणां सहस्रेषु कश्चिद्यतति सिद्धये ।
यततामपि सिद्धानां कश्चिन्मां वेत्ति तत्त्वतः ॥३॥

manuṣyāṇāṁ sahasreṣu
kaścid yatati siddhaye
yatatām api siddhānāṁ
kaścin māṁ vetti tattvataḥ

Of many thousands of people, one will attempt to reach perfection; of the few who reach this goal, only a rare soul will come to know Me as I am.

Mode *of* Goodness

Chapter 18, Verse 38

विषयेन्द्रियसंयोगाद्यत्तदग्रेऽमृतोपमम् ।
परिणामे विषमिव तत्सुखं राजसं स्मृतम् ॥३८॥

yat tad-agre viṣam iva
pariṇāme'mṛtopamam
tat sukhaṁ sāttvikaṁ proktam
ātma-buddhi-prasādajam

Happiness in the mode of goodness
may in the beginning seem like poison,
but at the end it is just like nectar, as it is
born out of the peace of self-realization.

God's Reciprocation

Chapter 4, Verse 11

ये यथा मां प्रपद्यन्ते तांस्तथैव भजाम्यहम् ।
मम वर्त्मानुवर्तन्ते मनुष्याः पार्थ सर्वशः ॥११॥

ye yathā māṁ prapadyante
tāṁs tathaiva bhajāmy aham
mama vartmānuvartante
manuṣyāḥ pārtha sarvaśaḥ

I reciprocate with all beings according to the way they surrender to Me. Everyone follows My path in all respects.

the Sage

Chapter 2, Verse 69

या निशा सर्वभूतानां तस्यां जागर्ति संयम ।
यस्यां जाग्रति भूतानि सा निशा पश्यतो मुनेः ॥६९॥

yā niśā sarva-bhūtānāṁ
tasyāṁ jāgarti saṁyamī
yasyāṁ jāgrati bhūtāni
sā niśā paśyato muneḥ

What is night for all creatures is the time of awakening for the self-controlled, and the time of awakening for all beings is night for the introspective sage.

Master *of* Mystics

Chapter 18, Verse 78

यत्र योगेश्वरः कृष्णो यत्र पार्थो धनुर्धरः ।
तत्र श्र विजयो भूतिर्ध्रुवा न तिर्मतिर्मम ॥७८॥

yatra yogeśvaraḥ kṛṣṇo
yatra pārtho dhanurdharaḥ
tatra śrīr vijayo bhūtir
dhruvā nītir matir mama

Wherever there is Krishna, the master of all mystics, and Arjuna, the supreme archer, there will always be opulence, victory, extraordinary power, and morality. I hold this to be true.

Wisdom and Leadership

Wisdom

Chapter 5, Verse 16

ज्ञानेन तु तदज्ञानं येषां नाशितमात्मनः ।
तेषामादित्यवज्ज्ञानं प्रकाशयति तत् परम् ॥१६॥

jñānena tu tad ajñānaṁ
yeṣāṁ nāśitam ātmanaḥ
teṣām ādityavaj jñānaṁ
prakāśayati tat-param

When one is illumined with the wisdom by which nescience is destroyed, then this knowledge lights up all things, just as the sun reveals the world at dawn.

True Leaders

Chapter 18, Verse 43

शौर्यं तेजो धृतिर्दाक्ष्यं युद्धे चाप्यपलायनम् ।
दानम श्वरभावश्च क्षात्रं कर्म स्वभावजम् ॥४३॥

śauryaṁ tejo dhṛtir dākṣyaṁ
yuddhe cāpy apalāyanam
dānam īśvara-bhāvaś ca
kṣātraṁ karma svabhāvajam

Heroism, power, determination, resourcefulness, courage in battle, generosity, and leadership are the natural qualities by which the *kshatriya* works.

Leadership

Chapter 3, Verse 21

यद्यदाचरति श्रेष्ठस्तत्तदेवेतरो जनः ।
स यत् प्रमाणं कुरुते लोकस्तदनुवर्तते ॥२१॥

yad yad ācarati śreṣṭhas
tat tad evetaro janaḥ
sa yat pramāṇaṁ kurute
lokas tad anuvartate

Whatever a great person does, common people follow. And whatever standards they set by exemplary acts, all the world pursues.

INFAMY

CHAPTER 2, VERSE 34

अक र्तिं चापि भूतानि कथयिष्यन्ति तेऽव्ययम् ।
सम्भावितस्य चाक र्तिर्मरणादतिरिच्यते ॥३४॥

akīrtiṁ cāpi bhūtāni
kathayiṣyanti te'vyayām
saṁbhāvitasya cākīrtir
maraṇād atiricyate

If you abandon your duty, all
will speak endlessly of your shameful
deed. For one who has been honored,
dishonor is worse than death.

Equal Vision

Chapter 5, Verse 18

विद्याविनयसम्पन्ने ब्राह्मणे गवि हस्तिनि ।
शुनि चैव श्वपाके च पण्डिताः समदर्शिनः ॥१८॥

vidyā-vinaya-sampanne
brāhmaṇe gavi hastini
śuni caiva śvapāke ca
paṇḍitāḥ sama-darśinaḥ

By virtue of transcendental knowledge, the wise see the same divine truth in all beings—from the wise and gentle priest to the cow, the elephant, the dog, or even the outcaste dog-eater.

Good Qualities

Chapter 18, Verse 42

शमो दमस्तपः शौचं क्षान्तिरार्जवमेव च ।
ज्ञानं विज्ञानमास्तिक्यं ब्रह्मकर्मस्वभावजम् ॥४२॥

śamo damas tapaḥ śaucaṁ
kṣāntir ārjavam eva ca
jñānaṁ vijñānam āstikyaṁ
brahma-karma svabhāvajam

The brahmin's work is born of his nature and qualities: peacefulness, self-control, asceticism, forgiveness, honesty, learning, wisdom, and a firm faith in the Supreme Lord.

Divine Descent

Chapter 4, Verses 7–8

यदा यदा हि धर्मस्य ग्लानिर्भवति भारत ।
अभ्युत्थानमधर्मस्य तदात्मानं सृजाम्यहम् ॥७॥

yadā yadā hi dharmasya
glānir bhavati bhārata
abhyutthānam adharmasya
tadātmānaṁ sṛjāmy aham

Whenever and wherever there is a decline of religious practice in the world and wickedness becomes predominant, at that time I descend Myself. In order to deliver the pious and to annihilate the miscreants, as well as to reestablish the sacred law, I appear in every age.

Lamp *of* Knowledge

Chapter 10, Verses 10–11

तेषां सततयुक्तानां भजतां प्र तिपूर्वकम् ।
ददामि बुद्धियोगं तं येन मामुपयान्ति ते ॥१०॥
तेषामेवानुकम्पार्थमहमज्ञानजं तमः ।
नाशयाम्यात्मभावस्थो ज्ञानद पेन भास्वता ॥११॥

teṣāṁ satata-yuktānāṁ
bhajatāṁ prīti-pūrvakam
dadāmi buddhi-yogaṁ taṁ
yena māṁ upayānti te

To those who are constantly devoted and worship Me with love, I give the intelligence by which they can attain Me. Out of compassion for them, dwelling in their hearts, I destroy the darkness of ignorance with the lamp of knowledge.

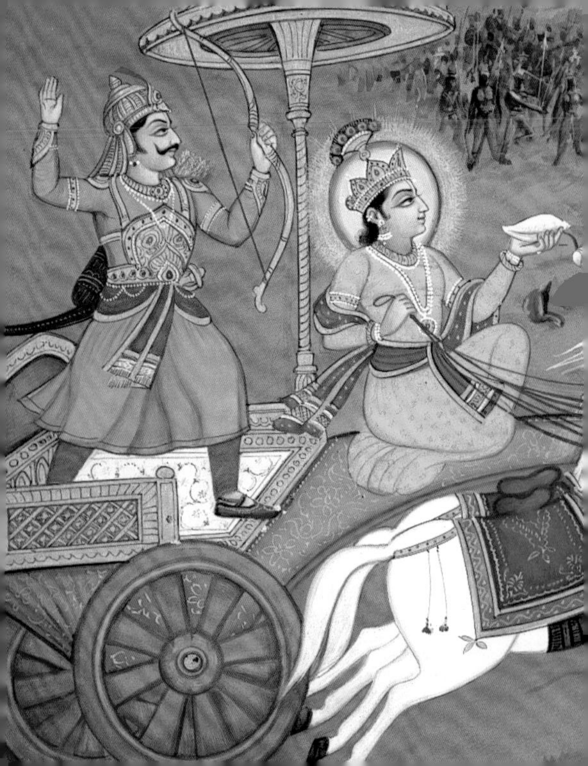

Birth and Death

the Time *of* Death

Chapter 8, Verses 5–6

अन्तकाले च मामेव स्मरन्मुक्त्वा कलेवरम् ।
यः प्रयाति स मद्भावं याति नास्त्यत्र संशयः ॥५॥
यं यं वापि स्मरन् भावं त्यजत्यन्ते कलेवरम् ।
तं तमेवैति कौन्तेय सदा तद्भावभावितः ॥६॥

anta-kāle ca mām eva
smaran muktvā kalevaram
yaḥ prayāti sa mad-bhāvaṁ
yāti nāsty atra saṁśayaḥ

At the time of death, whoever relinquishes the body, remembering Me alone, at once attains My nature. Of this there is no doubt. Whatever state of being one remembers when quitting the body will be attained without fail.

the DESTROYER

CHAPTER 10, VERSE 34

मृत्युः सर्वहरश्चाहमुद्भवश्च भविष्यताम् ।
कीर्तिः श्रीर्वाक्च नारीणां स्मृतिर्मेधा धृतिः क्षमा ॥३४॥

mṛtyuḥ sarva-haraś cāham
udbhavaś ca bhaviṣyatām
kīrtiḥ śrīr vāk ca nārīṇāṁ
smṛtir medhā dhṛtiḥ kṣamā

I am death, destroyer of all;
I am the source of all things yet to be.
Of women, I am fame, prosperity,
speech, memory, intelligence,
faithfulness, and patience.

Doubting Soul

Chapter 4, Verse 40

अज्ञश्चाश्रद्दधानश्च संशयात्मा विनश्यति ।
नायं लोकोऽस्ति न परो न सुखं संशयात्मनः ॥४०॥

ajñaś cāśraddadhānaś ca
saṁśayātmā vinaśyati
nāyaṁ loko'sti na paro
na sukhaṁ saṁśayātmanaḥ

But the ignorant and faithless person who doubts the truth will forever be lost. The doubting soul is happy neither in this life, or the next.

Higher Realms

Chapter 8, Verse 16

आब्रह्मभुवनाल्लोकाः पुनरावर्तिनोऽर्जुन ।
मामुपेत्य तु कौन्तेय पुनर्जन्म न विद्यते ॥१६॥

ā brahma-bhuvanāl lokāḥ
punar-āvartino'rjuna
mām upetya tu kaunteya
punar-janma na vidyate

From the highest sphere in the material world down to the lowest, all are places of misery where birth and death take place. But whoever joins Me in My abode is never born again, O son of Kunti!

Eternal Soul

Chapter 2, Verse 20

न जायते म्रियते वा कदाचि-
न्नायं भूत्वा भविता वा न भूयः ।
अजो नित्यः शाश्वतोऽयं पुराणो
न हन्यते हन्यमाने शर रे ॥२०॥

na jāyate mriyate vā kadācin
nāyaṁ bhūtvā bhavitā vā na bhūyaḥ
ajo nityaḥ śāśvato'yaṁ purāṇo
na hanyate hanyamāne śarīre

For the soul there is neither birth nor death. The soul that is will never cease to be. It is unborn, eternal, ever-existing, undying, and primeval. It is not slain when the body is slain.

Grief

Chapter 2, Verse 11

श्र भगवानुवाच
अशोच्यानन्वशोचस्त्वं प्रज्ञावादांश्च भाषसे ।
गतासूनगतासूंश्च नानुशोचन्ति पण्डिताः ॥११॥

aśocyān anvaśocas tvaṁ
prajñā-vādāṁś ca bhāṣase
gatāsūn agatāsūṁś ca
nānuśocanti paṇḍitāḥ

You are mourning when there is no cause to lament, and yet you speak words that seem to be wise. The truly wise lament neither for the living nor the dead.

Great Souls

Chapter 7, Verse 19

बहूनां जन्मनामन्ते ज्ञानवान् मां प्रपद्यते ।
वासुदेवः सर्वमिति स महात्मा सुदुर्लभः ॥१९॥

bahūnāṁ janmanām ante
jñānavān māṁ prapadyate
vāsudevaḥ sarvam iti
sa mahātmā sudurlabhaḥ

After innumerable births
and deaths, those who are wise
surrender unto Me, knowing Me to
be the cause of all causes and all that
exists. Such great souls are very rare.

Changing Bodies

Chapter 2, Verse 22

वासांसि ज र्णानि यथा विहाय
नवानि गृह्णाति नरोऽपराणि ।
तथा शर राणि विहाय ज र्णा-
न्यन्यानि संयाति नवानि देह ॥२२॥

vāsāṁsi jīrṇāni yathā vihāya
navāni gṛhṇāti naro'parāṇi
tathā śarīrāṇi vihāya jīrṇāni
anyāni saṁyāti navāni dehī

As a person puts on new garments, giving up old ones, the soul similarly accepts new material bodies, giving up the old and used ones.

Transmigration

Chapter 2, Verse 13

देहिनोऽस्मिन्यथा देहे कौमारं यौवनं जरा ।
तथा देहान्तरप्राप्तिधीरस्तत्र न मुह्यति ॥१३॥

dehino'smin yathā dehe
kaumāraṁ yauvanaṁ jarā
tathā dehāntara-prāptir
dhīras tatra na muhyati

As the embodied soul continuously passes in this body, from childhood to youth to old age, the soul similarly passes into another body at death. Such a change does not disturb the minds of those who know the truth.

Rebirth

Chapter 2, Verse 27

जातस्य हि ध्रुवो मृत्युर्ध्रुवं जन्म मृतस्य च ।
तस्मादपरिहार्येऽर्थे न त्वं शोचितुमर्हसि ॥२७॥

jātasya hi dhruvo mṛtyur
dhruvaṁ janma mṛtasya ca
tasmād aparihārye'rthe
na tvaṁ śocitum arhasi

For one who is born, death is certain; for one who has died, birth is certain. As you cannot avoid either fate, you should not lament.